Draw Yourself at
100 Years Old

Jonathon Phillips

Photographs by Lindsay Edwards

Draw Yourself at 100 Years Old

Text: Jonathon Phillips
Publishers: Tania Mazzeo and Eliza Webb
Series consultant: Amanda Sutera
  Hands on Heads Consulting
Editor: Laken Ballinger
Project editor: Annabel Smith
Designer: Leigh Ashforth
Project designer: Danielle Maccarone
Permissions researcher: Liz McShane
Production controller: Renee Tome

Acknowledgements

All photographs by Lindsay Edwards Photography © Cengage Learning
Australia Pty Limited, except those listed below.

We would like to thank the following for permission to reproduce
copyright material:

p. 4 (left): iStock.com/MEDITERRANEAN, (right): Shutterstock.com/Claudia
Paulussen; p. 7 (bottom), back cover (middle): iStock.com/joka2000; p. 9
(bottom): Shutterstock.com/MintraTH; p. 10 (bottom): Shutterstock.
com/Peter Kotoff; p. 11 (bottom): iStock.com/Jeremy Poland; p. 12
(bottom), back cover (left): Shutterstock.com/sirtravelalot; p. 13 (top
right): Shutterstock.com/imranahmedsg; p. 15 (bottom right), back cover
(right): iStock.com/EMPPhotography; p. 17 (bottom): iStock.com/Goodboy
Picture Company; p. 18 (bottom right): Shutterstock.com/Fotoluminate
LLC; p. 19 (bottom right): iStock.com/Goodboy Picture Company; p. 21
(right): iStock.com/Leylaynr

Every effort has been made to trace and acknowledge copyright.
However, if any infringement has occurred, the publishers tender their
apologies and invite the copyright holders to contact them.

NovaStar

Text © 2024 Cengage Learning Australia Pty Limited

ISBN 978 0 17 033402 0

Cengage Learning Australia
Level 5, 80 Dorcas Street
Southbank VIC 3006 Australia
Phone: 1300 790 853
Email: aust.nelsonprimary@cengage.com

For learning solutions, visit **cengage.com.au**

Printed in China by 1010 Printing International Ltd
1 2 3 4 5 6 7 28 27 26 25 24

*Nelson acknowledges the Traditional Owners and Custodians
of the lands of all First Nations Peoples. We pay respect
to Elders past and present, and extend that respect to
all First Nations Peoples today.*

Contents

Our Changing Faces 〰〰〰

Have you ever wondered what you might look like when you are 100 years old? Do you think your nose will be the same size and shape? Will you have less hair, or more?

One thing is for sure, the face you see in the mirror today will be *very* different from the one that you will see when you are 100 years old!

Find out how our faces change over time, and follow the steps to draw yourself at 100 years old!

Goal

To draw yourself at 100 years old

Materials

You will need:

an A3 sheet of paper

a pencil

a ruler

an eraser

a black marker

Steps

Head

1. Start by drawing your head. Use the pencil to draw a large oval on the sheet of paper.

AS WE GET OLDER ...

Our faces change from a round to a more oval shape.

2 Next, add some **guidelines**. These are lines that will help you draw the different parts of your face in the right spots. Use the ruler to draw one **horizontal** line across the middle of the oval. Then, draw a **vertical** line through the middle.

You will erase these lines later, so draw them lightly.

Eyes

3 Just below the horizontal guideline, draw two almond shapes for eyes. Our eyes are usually one eye-width apart, so leave a space about the same size as another almond between your eyes.

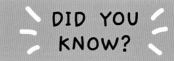

DID YOU KNOW?

An almond is a kind of nut. Human eyes are often said to be shaped like almonds.

4 Next, add an **iris** in each eye. Draw a pair of brackets inside each almond shape.

5 Add a **pupil** to each eye. Inside each pair of brackets (the irises), draw a small black circle.

⟩ DID YOU KNOW? ⟨

The iris is the coloured part of the eye, and the pupil is the dark spot in the middle.

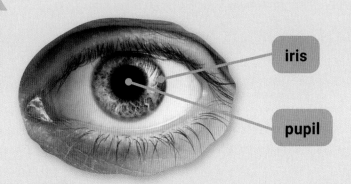

iris

pupil

6 Under each eye, draw some upward curving lines to make some saggy eye "bags".

AS WE GET OLDER ...

Our eyes do not change size, but the skin around them can **sag** and make our eyes look smaller.

7 Next, add some crow's feet. Draw a few small lines curving out from the outside corner of each eye.

AS WE GET OLDER ...

More lines, or wrinkles, appear on the outside edges of our eyes, and they are much longer than before. These lines are sometimes called "crow's feet".

8 Last, add the eyebrows along the horizontal guideline. Make them by drawing two long lines across your face using very short **diagonal** lines to look like hair.

AS WE GET OLDER ...

The hair in our eyebrows gets thicker and longer.

Nose

9 Start the nose by using the ruler to draw a new guideline halfway between the horizontal guideline and the bottom of your face.

10 Next, draw the end of your nose. Put a wide letter "U" shape just below the middle of the new guideline. Make it about the same width as the gap between your eyes. Then, draw two smaller letter "U"s at either end, curved up to the guideline, for your nostrils.

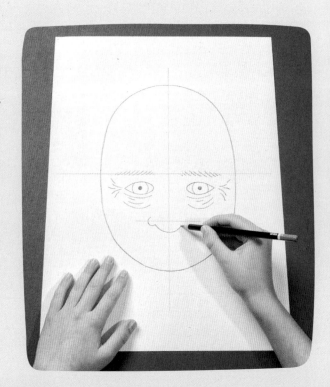

11 Finish by adding some **laugh lines** going from each side of your nose in a downwards direction.

AS WE GET OLDER ...

Our nose grows larger and looks like it is lower on our face.

Mouth

12 Begin the mouth by drawing where your top and bottom lip meet. Put a slightly wavy line halfway between your nose and the bottom of your face. Make it about as wide as your nose.

13 Add some wrinkles around your mouth. Along the wavy line, draw six short lines going up and down, both above and below it.

Then, at each end of your mouth, draw a small wavy line that goes downwards towards the bottom of your face.

Finally, draw a short wobbly line for your bottom lip.

AS WE GET OLDER ...

We get small, thin wrinkles around our lips and at the sides of our mouths.

Ears

14 Next, add your ears. Draw a line that curves outwards and down on each side of your head. Start at about the same height as the horizontal guideline, and finish at the height of your nose.

AS WE GET OLDER ...
Our ears get longer!

Neck and Shoulders

15 For your shoulders, draw two lines that curve downwards, starting from the middle of each ear to the side edges of the paper.

16 Then, draw some sagging skin around your neck by adding a few long wobbly lines under your chin.

AS WE GET OLDER ...

The muscles in our neck get weaker. This makes us look like our head is sinking into our shoulders!

Hair

17 Now, think about what your hair might look like when you are 100 years old. Will it be curly or straight? Perhaps you will have no hair at all!

Once you have chosen your hairstyle, start drawing your hair around your head by adding some lines going in a downwards direction.

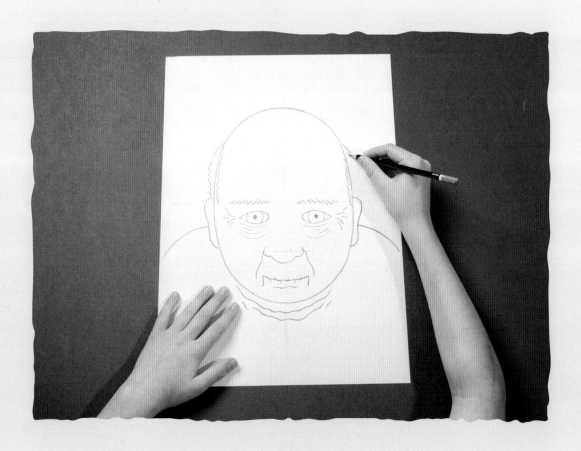

Remember to draw lightly so that you can erase any lines if they do not look right.

18 Finally, think about some extra things to add to your 100-year-old self. For example, you could add more wrinkles by drawing four wavy lines across your **forehead**, and two wavy lines down each cheek.

You could also add some glasses, some jewellery or some extra hair growing out of your nose and ears!

AS WE GET OLDER ...

Our hair becomes thinner. Some people even lose their hair.

19 To finish, use the black marker to **trace** over the lines you want to keep. Then, rub out the guidelines and other pencil marks with the eraser.

You now have a **glimpse** into your future – a picture of yourself at 100 years old!

Glossary

forehead (*noun*)	the part of the face above the eyes
diagonal (*adjective*)	lines going in a slanted direction
glimpse (*noun*)	a small look, seeing something for a short time
guidelines (*noun*)	a set of lines to mark the space to draw in
horizontal (*adjective*)	lining up with the ground and not up and down
iris (*noun*)	the round part in an eye that is coloured
laugh lines (*noun*)	folds or wrinkles between the mouth and nose
pupil (*noun*)	the small black round area in the middle of the eye
sag (*verb*)	droop or hang down
trace (*verb*)	draw by following the line of something
vertical (*adjective*)	up and down, not lining up with the ground

Index